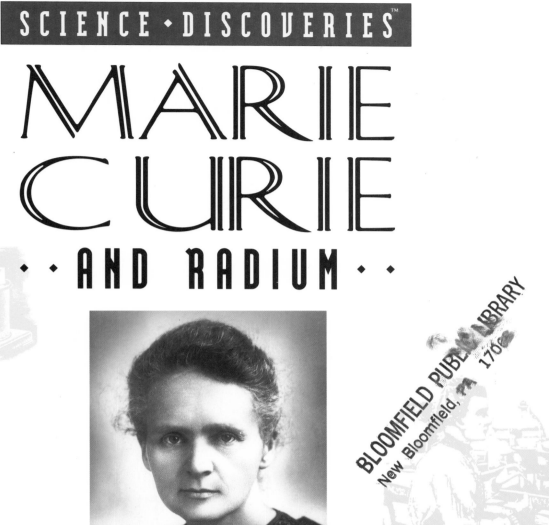

SCIENCE · DISCOVERIES™

MARIE CURIE

· AND RADIUM · ·

STEVE · PARKER

HarperCollinsPublishers

Acknowledgements

Photographic credits:
AIP Niels Bohr Library: 11 bottom right, Lande Collection; 19 bottom, UK Atomic Energy Authority
Barnaby's Picture Library, 22
Bridgeman Art Library, 8 bottom
Mary Evans Picture Library, 11 top, 15 bottom left
L'Illustration/Sygma, 16 bottom left, 24 top, 26 bottom
Musée Curie, Paris, title page, 8 top, 9 right, 17 top, 26 top
Popperfoto/Marie Curie Collection, 2, 5 top and bottom, 6, 9 left, 10 top and bottom, 12 top and bottom, 13, 16 top and middle right, 19 top, 20 top and bottom, 23, 24 bottom, 25
Science Photo Library: 4, Martin Bond; 11, 15 bottom left, J-L Charmet; 15 top, Martin Bond; bottom right, Alexander Tsiaras; 17 bottom, J-L Charmet; 27 top, Los Alamos National Laboratory; 27 bottom, J-L Charmet

Cover montage images supplied by Mary Evans Picture Library and Ann Ronan Picture Library

Illustrations:
Tony Smith, 6–7, 14, 22–23
Rodney Shackell, 13, 18, 21, 25

Marie Curie and Radium

Printed in Hong Kong for Imago Publishing

1   2   3   4   5   6   7   8   9   10

Library of Congress Cataloging-in-Publication Data
Parker, Steve.
   Marie Curie and radium / Steve Parker.
      p.   cm. — (Science discoveries)
   Includes index.
   Summary: Details the life and work of Marie Curie from early childhood to the discovery of radium and her two Nobel Prizes.
   ISBN 0-06-020847-3 ISBN 0-06-021472-4 (lib. bdg.)
   1. Curie, Marie, 1867–1934—Juvenile literature.
2. Chemists—France—Biography—Juvenile literature.
3. Radium—Juvenile literature.   4. Chemists.
   [1. Curie, Marie, 1867-1934.]   I. Title.   II. Series.
QD22.C8P37   1992   92-3616
540′.92—dc20   CIP
[B]   AC

This statue of Marie Curie is in Warsaw, the city of her childhood.

Contents

Introduction

The 20th century has been called the Atomic Age. As it began, scientists were trying to find out if atoms, which they had thought were the smallest particles of a substance, were made up of even smaller particles. They succeeded in splitting the atom in 1919. This knowledge has produced the terrifying weapon of the atomic bomb. It has also led to atomic or nuclear power, with its benefits and drawbacks.

Marie Curie's work with radioactive elements provided the foundation for the Atomic Age. She discovered the element radium, which naturally gives off radioactivity as its atoms split apart. Marie Curie carried out her research at a time when the nature of radioactivity was not understood at all. She also had to struggle with lack of money and recognition, against illness, and against those who mistakenly believed that a woman could not be a real scientist.

Eventually Marie Curie became world famous and won two Nobel Prizes. Today she is considered one of the great pioneers of science.

Marie Curie's research was an important building block toward the splitting of the atom, which produces nuclear energy. Today, nuclear power stations like the one below generate huge quantities of electricity.

Chapter One

The Early Years

Maria Sklodowska was born at this site, 16 Freta Street, Warsaw. The building has been converted to a museum in memory of her life and work.

On November 7, 1867, a baby girl was born on Freta Street in Warsaw, Poland. She was named Maria Salomee Sklodowska, though her family would call her Manya (her name is sometimes written Marya Sklodovska). Her parents were teachers in Warsaw. They already had four children: daughters Sofia, Bronislawa (Bronia), and Helena, and son Jozef.

The Sklodowska children. Maria was the youngest of the family. Oldest sister Sofia is on the left, with brother Jozef sitting on the table.

At the time, Poland was under the rule of neighboring Russia. The best educations and the best jobs went to Russians. Most Polish people were poor, and their lives were hard. However, with two teachers as parents, Maria and her family were better off than many others.

Maria (on the left), her father, and her two surviving sisters. (Sofia died in 1876.) This photograph was taken just before Bronia (to the right of her father) left to study in Paris.

· *Family life in Warsaw*

The children had a good education. They were brought up strictly and encouraged to work hard, to respect their elders, and to be religious. They had caring parents, but they noticed that their mother suddenly stopped kissing or even hugging them. She had caught the then incurable disease of tuberculosis and did not want to pass the germs to her children. In 1876, Maria's oldest sister, Sofia, died of typhus. Two years later their mother died.

In 1883, Maria finished her school education. She had shown herself to be a hard worker, and very clever. She was able to concentrate on her work and had a very good memory. She won a gold medal at her school, the Russian Lycée. But she became ill with what she called "the fatigue of growth and study" and spent a year recovering with relatives in the country.

On her return to Warsaw, Maria and her sister Bronia began to attend secret meetings of the "Floating University." The members read about scientific and other work that was banned by the Russians who thought it might stir up rebellious ideas. In 1885, to help with family finances, Maria became a governess.

When Maria traveled from Warsaw to Paris, she took everything she would need—including a stove, and even parts of her bed.

Pupil and teacher

Maria worked for several families, teaching and looking after the children. In her spare time, she taught herself math and physics. She sent some of her wages to her sister Bronia, who had gone to Paris to study medicine. (Later, Bronia would help Maria with money for her studies.)

In 1890, her father obtained a better job, and the family's money worries lessened. Maria lived with him for a while and also taught the sciences. She began to consider going to the University of Paris, like her sister, since Warsaw University did not admit women. And so in 1891, Maria Sklodowska went to Paris by third-class train, to study for math and physics degrees.

Great thinkers of the time

Maria read the works of many scientists and other famous thinkers, even though the Russians tried to ban them in Poland.

• The English naturalist Charles Darwin had written about evolution and the struggle for survival in his book *On the Origin of Species* (1859). His work led many scientists to doubt the existence of a God, and this greatly affected Maria.

• The French thinker Auguste Comte wrote *Positive Philosophy* in the 1830s and 1840s. Maria and her friends in the Floating University called themselves "positivists," since Comte's philosophy fitted in with their hopes of getting rid of the Russians and leaving Poland free.

• Maria also studied how scientists should think clearly and logically, carry out experiments, and test their ideas and theories. By her middle teens, she was no longer religious. Her scientific mind could not believe in something that could not be proved. Eventually science would replace religion and politics in Maria's life.

Maria worked hard while at the university. Her French was not good, and she had only a small circle of friends. She rarely enjoyed the stylish Paris lifestyle shown in the painting below, by Edmond Georges Grandjean.

Chapter Two
Paris

At first, Maria stayed with Bronia and Bronia's doctor husband in Paris. But she soon moved to the area where students often lived in Paris, living in a tiny dark attic with only a coal stove for heat. She had very little money, ate poorly, and worked long hours in the library. Yet she found her work so satisfying that the hardships were worthwhile.

Maria studied at the Sorbonne (part of the University of Paris) under some of the most famous mathematicians and physicists of the time, including Paul Appel and Gabriel Lippmann. In 1893, she received her physics degree. She earned the highest marks in her group and began to work in Lippmann's laboratory. The next year she received her math degree, placing second in her group. Now she planned to do pure scientific research, for the love of her subject and the joy of increased knowledge, rather than for any money that could be made from it.

Pierre Curie

Pierre Curie was born in 1859 in Paris and educated by his father, a physician. Even as a schoolboy of 14, he was deeply interested in mathematics. In 1878, he became a laboratory assistant at the University of Paris. With his brother Jacques, he studied heat, crystals, magnetism, and electricity. Four years later, he became supervisor at the École de Physique (School of Physics).

The Curies prepare for a bicycle ride from the garden of their house on Boulevard Kellerman. Cycling was one of their many shared loves.

Research and marriage

At the age of 27, Maria met Pierre Curie at the home of a Polish physicist. He was 35, a senior worker in a physics laboratory. They had much in common, including a love of nature and the countryside, little desire for wealth and the comforts of life, and a great passion for physics research.

Pierre wrote letters of love and physics experiments to Maria. The next year, on July 26, 1895, they were married in Sceaux, Pierre's hometown near Paris. Maria Sklodowska became Marie Curie. Their honeymoon was the first of their many bicycle trips around France, during which they enjoyed the fresh air and countryside and recovered from their long hours in labs and libraries.

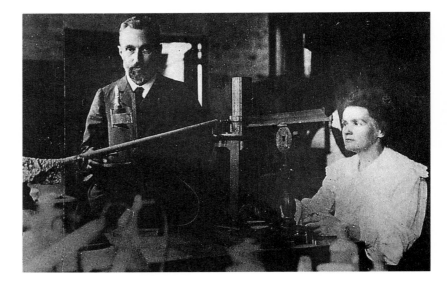

Pierre and Marie photographed in their laboratory in 1898. This was about the time she was purifying uranium ore to find the mystery radioactive substance.

On September 12, 1897, Irène Curie was born. A few months after she was born, Marie published her first scientific work—her report on the magnetic properties of steel.

The Curies at work

Both Marie and Pierre loved their research for the way it advanced scientific knowledge. Pierre had worked his way up through various jobs helping in laboratories, not as a student. He published his important findings regularly in scientific journals, but he did not try to sell them to make money from them, and he refused payments and loans for research. Despite his scientific successes, the university superiors did not choose him for a more important post because, in their view, he did not have the proper qualifications, such as a science degree. In 1895, however, Pierre Curie did receive a doctor of science degree for his earlier work on magnetism.

Marie went to work with Pierre at the École de Physique after their marriage. She studied the magnetic properties of various alloys, and wrote the first of her dozens of scientific publications.

Rays and radiation

Meanwhile, in November 1895, Wilhelm Roentgen, a German physicist, discovered invisible "penetrating rays" coming from an electric tube in one of his experiments. He called them X rays, because he did not know what they were. They could pass through flesh and other soft substances, but not through hard, dense materials like bone and thick metals.

X rays and their effects became world famous within months. Marie and Pierre Curie followed the new discoveries about these "strange emissions" with interest, as they studied and prepared lectures at their plainly furnished apartment on the Rue de la Glacière.

In 1896, the French physicist Henri Becquerel discovered more kinds of penetrating rays. Unlike Roentgen's, which were made by an electrical effect, these rays seemed to come naturally from a piece of uranium. Becquerel had left the uranium lying on a sealed packet of photographic paper for several days in a drawer, and it caused the paper to mist over. Marie, looking for a new subject to study for her doctor of science degree, chose the mysterious rays detected by Becquerel.

X rays caused much interest, and even amusement, as their "see-through" qualities became known to the public. This cartoon was published in 1900, five years after their discovery.

A new kind of ray

Wilhelm Roentgen (above) discovered X rays while working as a professor of physics at the University of Würzburg, Germany. He told hardly anyone about his findings for two months, as he worked day and night trying to make sense of the discovery. One of the first X-ray images (below) was of his wife's hand and ring. Roentgen was awarded the first Nobel Prize for Physics, in 1901.

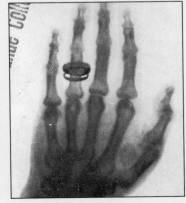

Marie spent most of her time working hard in her "shed" behind the main physics buildings at the University of Paris.

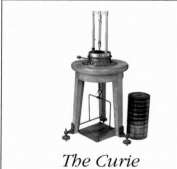

The Curie electrometer

Pierre and Jacques Curie invented their electrometer to find out whether a substance was giving off emissions or not. When a substance gives off radioactive emissions, the air around it carries electricity. This electricity is measured by the electrometer.

Chapter Three

The Discovery of Radium

For her laboratory, Marie was offered a small, damp, unheated room in the École de Physique. She had no money for her research, and she worked with equipment and materials given to her by colleagues.

Using the electrometer invented by Pierre and his brother Jacques, she began to look for other substances that gave off emissions as uranium did. She discovered that a substance called thorium also gave off emissions. She found that it did not matter how uranium or substances containing it were treated— they always gave off the same amount of emissions.

Marie reasoned that the emissions could not be caused by chemical reactions; otherwise they would change as the uranium was added to or separated from other chemicals. Could they be coming from the smallest particles of uranium itself—its atoms? This idea went against all the scientific theories of the time, but it proved to be true. Marie and Pierre also became interested in the luminous effects of the newly discovered emissions, since they caused certain substances to glow.

Too many emissions

Marie's main source of uranium was an ore called pitchblende. The mineral chalcolite also contained uranium. In 1898, her tests and calculations showed that pitchblende and chalcolite gave off more emissions than expected from the amount of uranium they contained. There must be another substance in the ore mixture that gave off the extra emissions.

Finding the mystery substance

Marie began the chemical procedures to find the mystery substance. It was hard physical work. She ground the ore, sieved it, dissolved it by boiling, boiled off the liquid, filtered it, distilled it, and electrolyzed it. She and her colleagues checked the contents and purity at each stage.

After each stage, Marie took the part that gave off the most emissions and purified it further. Finally she arrived at a pure version of the new substance, which was a metal—a new chemical element. In great excitement she called it polonium, after her homeland of Poland. In the scientific report of her work, she invented the word *radioactive* to describe substances such as uranium and polonium that gave off penetrating rays or radiation.

A page from one of Marie's laboratory notebooks, containing mathematical equations about energy emissions.

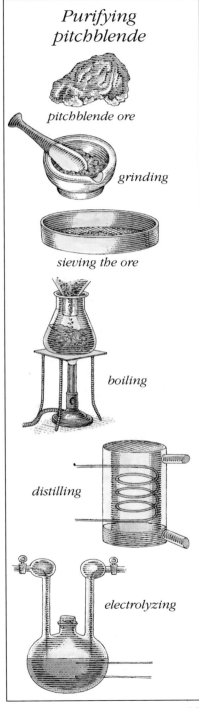

Purifying pitchblende

pitchblende ore

grinding

sieving the ore

boiling

distilling

electrolyzing

Glowing in the dark

Polonium was the first highly radioactive element to be isolated in pure form. It gave off so much radiation, it made the surrounding air glow, and the polonium itself became hot.

But Marie's work had shown that polonium, though powerful, was not responsible for the rest of the pitchblende's radioactivity. She continued her work and partly purified a substance that she thought contained another new element. This she named radium, after the Latin word *radius*, meaning "ray." However, there was so little of it in the pitchblende that huge amounts of ore would be needed to prepare a tiny pure sample of radium.

Some of the radioactive substances purified by the Curies gave off an eerie glow. Pierre kept a small glass container of one of them in his pocket and brought it out at gatherings as a party trick. Guests were amazed by the unearthly light.

The search for radium

In 1899, Marie began the immense task of obtaining pure radium in some form, in order to prove its existence. Pierre was still lecturing and working on his own research, but he gradually became more and more interested in radioactivity. His chief task was to analyze the samples that Marie made at each stage of the process.

Tons of radioactive mine wastes arrived at the Paris lab, from Bohemia (now part of Czechoslovakia) and the Belgian Congo (now Zaire) in Africa. Marie performed the chemical separation processes on bucketfuls of it. The final stages were difficult and often unsuccessful.

At the time, the hazards of working with radioactive materials were not fully known. For most of her adult life, Marie suffered ill health. She had the symptoms of tuberculosis after her daughter Irène's birth, and soon she was sick, tired, and aching because of radiation poisoning. Her hands became stiff, cracked, and ulcer covered as she mixed and boiled the radioactive materials. Even many years later, her notebooks and laboratory seat were highly radioactive.

It is remarkable that Marie was able to carry out such hard physical work, even with her long cycling breaks in the countryside. It is also remarkable that she lived so long. Many of her colleagues died much younger.

Danger! Radioactive!

Today we are aware of the hazards of radioactivity (above is the international warning symbol). In Marie Curie's time, the hazards were just beginning to be revealed. Both Curies refused to believe that radiation was dangerous. Marie accepted the dangers only toward the end of her life. Today people wear protective clothing (see below) when working with radioactive materials.

The Curie family in a rare moment of relaxation. Both Marie and Pierre often looked tired and ill from long periods of work and exposure to radioactivity.

15

Chapter Four
First Woman of Science

In later life, Marie Curie described the hard years of purifying radium as the best of her life. She looked after her family and home, but her research took up most of her time. Among her helpers were André Debierne (one of Pierre's students) and Gustave Bémont. She was a thorough worker and demanded high standards of cleanliness from her assistants in the laboratory—the "shed" behind the École de Physique.

While she was studying radium, Marie carried out other research. In 1899, with Henri Becquerel and another scientist, Fritz Giesel, she investigated the properties of the emissions themselves. Pierre became more interested in this part of the research.

Marie worked enormously hard in her laboratory and workshop at the Rue Lhomond, shown on the right. She was often tired, felt sick, and had pain in her joints and muscles. She suffered sore hands from radiation burns caused by the substances she worked with. At first, she and Pierre thought these problems were due to the very long hours they spent on their research.

◀ *The French physicist Henri Becquerel, here standing next to a huge electromagnet, worked closely with the Curies. In 1896, he discovered the radioactive emissions of uranium, and together they showed that the beta rays or beta particles (see page 21) given off by radium were really streams of electrons, moving at high speed. Becquerel's work also led to the invention of the fluorescent light, and a unit of measurement in radiation physics is named after him.*

One tenth of a gram

The next year, the Curies moved to Boulevard Kellerman in Paris. Eugène, Pierre's father, joined them to help care for Irène. Pierre discontinued his crystal research and began to study the properties of the radioactive emissions.

To help with the family income and provide money for their research, Marie and Pierre both took extra jobs. She became a physics lecturer at an academy for girls in Sèvres. He took the additional post of Assistant Professor at the Polytechnique. Despite the Curies' increasing reputations in the scientific world and their many achievements, the University of Paris was very slow to recognize their work, and still provided no money for their research.

During the early 1900s, the Curies sent samples of their purified radioactive substances to laboratories in other countries. As a result, research on radioactivity leaped forward and many other scientists became involved.

Eventually, in 1902, Marie made a pure form of radium. There was only 0.1 gram—a small speck. (Seven tons of pitchblende yield 1 gram of radium.) Yet it was enough radium to use in defining some of its physical and chemical properties. She announced the results of her work to her scientific colleagues. It was the peak of her research career.

The Curies in the garden of their house on Boulevard Kellerman, Paris. They enjoyed growing flowers and watching birds there. By this time, Marie and Pierre were famous scientists, as shown by the cover of the illustrated magazine below, from 1904. A feature in the magazine describes the discovery of radium.

17

The *"light fairy"*

In 1904, an American dancer in Paris, Loie Fuller, used electric lights (then still unfamiliar) to make her costume glow. She wrote to Marie for some radium to give the same effect. Marie refused, but she was fascinated by the idea. The "light fairy" Loie came to dance for the Curies in their living room—after her team of electricians rigged up her costume. Baby Ève was enchanted, and Marie and Loie became friends.

Rewards and awards

The next year, Pierre was persuaded to put his name forward for election to the French Academy of Science. But he was not elected. The French still did not recognize the significance of the Curies' work, though their fame was growing abroad.

Pierre was invited to speak at the Royal Institution in London, where he and Marie were treated as important guests. While in Britain, Marie became friendly with Hertha Ayrton, the Polish wife of an English professor. She also met another world-famous physicist, Ernest Rutherford, the leader of the team that later split the atom. With Pierre, she was awarded the Davy Medal by the Royal Society of London. Back in Paris, Marie at last received her doctor of science degree.

There were disappointments. Marie became pregnant a second time, but the baby died shortly after birth. There was no way of knowing at the time that radioactivity might harm a baby—today recognized as one of its most serious hazards. Pierre applied to become a professor of mineralogy at the Sorbonne, but again he was unsuccessful.

A Nobel Prize

The same year, Marie and Pierre Curie and Henri Becquerel were awarded the third Nobel Prize for Physics ever given, for their work on radioactivity. Sadly, though not surprisingly, neither of the Curies felt well enough to attend the ceremony in Sweden.

Their feelings about the prize were mixed. Marie was proud of her work and proud to be the first woman to achieve world fame as a scientist. As a woman, she had always believed in equality with men, but she did not join with the feminists and suffragettes who were fighting for women's rights at the time. The Nobel Prize money also helped to fund their research, which they had so far paid for by themselves. But the fame interfered with their beloved work.

The first radium factory was set up at Noget-sur-Marne in France. Pure radium is a metal, lustrous white in appearance. Hailed as a wonder substance at first, its dangers were gradually recognized as people working with it or using it became ill and died.

New Zealand-born Ernest Rutherford was a foremost scientist in England during the early 20th century. He led the teams that put forward the theory of the atom's structure in 1911 and split the atom in 1919. His work built on the Curies' research.

Success and tragedy

In 1904, the Curies' daughter Éve was born and Pierre at last became a professor at the Sorbonne. He had a better laboratory, and Marie was his paid chief assistant. The next year, he was elected to the Academy of Sciences.

Marie's great discovery, radium, was becoming famous. People were intrigued by its property of glowing in the dark. It was also used to cure certain diseases.

As radium's possible uses became clear, its value rocketed. Manufacturers wrote to the Curies, offering them huge amounts of money for radium, or for the purifying methods. But the Curies refused to make money in this way, even though they had to ask for donations to set up their own Radium Institute. Nevertheless, radium manufacturers, clinics, and factories sprang up around the world.

On April 19, 1906, tragedy struck. Pierre was lost in thought as he walked along a Paris street and stepped out in front of a heavy horse-drawn wagon. He was crushed under its wheels and killed.

Chapter Five
Setting New Standards

Marie was devastated by Pierre's death. She wrote love letters to him as his body lay in the house awaiting burial. To escape her grief, within a month she was back at work. She was offered and accepted Pierre's job and became the first woman to lecture at the Sorbonne. In 1908, she became the university's first female professor.

Marie had found a house in Pierre's hometown of Sceaux, near Paris, for her daughters and father-in-law. She employed a Polish cousin as a governess and taught her daughters herself for a time. The shy Irène, like her mother, took to mathematics and science. The more confident Éve was gifted in painting, music, and other creative arts.

Marie with her daughters Irène (on the right) and Éve. The children studied for one hour each day with their mother. Later they attended a private school with the children of other professors. The parents took turns giving lessons.

The certificate for Marie's Nobel Prize for Chemistry.

A second Nobel Prize

Lord Kelvin, a Scottish physicist, suggested that radium was not an element, since it had been found to give off helium gas, which is itself an element. (Today we know that helium nuclei are the same thing as alpha particles, which was the reason for Lord Kelvin's confusing discovery.) So Marie continued to make even purer polonium and radium. By 1910, she had produced pure radium and shown that it was a brilliant-white metal. She even found its melting point, 1292°F (700°C).

The same year, Marie published her 971-page work, *Traité de Radioactivité (Treatise on Radioactivity)*. In 1911, came another great honor—the Nobel Prize for Chemistry, awarded to Marie alone for isolating pure radium.

The curie

Marie Curie proposed the adoption of a standard unit of radioactivity, related to the emissions from one gram of radium. Today the same international unit is used—the curie. One curie is the amount of a radioactive substance in which 37,000 million atoms change, or decay, every second.

Atoms and radioactivity

An atom is like our solar system, in which planets go around the sun—but much smaller! The biggest atom is far too small to be seen under even the most powerful microscope.

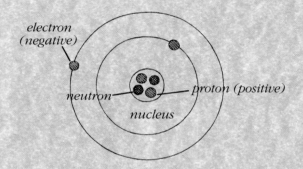

electron (negative)
neutron
proton (positive)
nucleus

- The central part of the atom (the "sun") is the nucleus. It has two primary kinds of particles. These are protons, which have a positive electrical charge, and neutrons, which are neutral—neither positive nor negative.

- The particles going around the nucleus (the "planets") are electrons. They are negatively charged. Normally the numbers of electrons and protons are equal, so the negatives and positives balance.

- Each chemical element, such as oxygen or carbon or radium, has its own special number of protons, neutrons, and electrons.

Radioactivity is the spontaneous disintegration of atomic nuclei by emission of atomic particles and/or electromagnetic radiation. As the radioactivity is given off, the substance changes, or decays, into a different element. There are three main types of radioactivity.

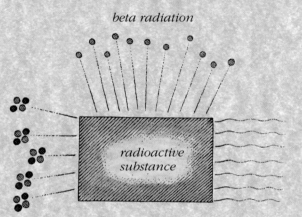

beta radiation
radioactive substance
alpha radiation
gamma radiation

- Alpha particles. Each is made of two protons and two neutrons.

- Beta particles are electrons that have a high energy level and are emitted by the nuclei of radioactive atoms. They are 7,000 times smaller than alpha particles.

- Gamma rays are electromagnetic radiation. Gamma rays are not particles but waves like light or X rays. They are so small and energetic that they may pass right through a substance.

Different radioactive substances give off different proportions of the three types. The different kinds of radium, between them, give off all three kinds of radiation.

Suffragettes

The late 19th and early 20th centuries saw the growth of the suffragette movement in Europe and America. Many women (and men) campaigned for the right of all women to vote, since in most countries only men could vote. Marie Curie was not actively involved, but her achievements and awards were a great encouragement. This photograph shows one of the most famous British suffragettes, Emmeline Pankhurst, being arrested in London in 1914.

A troubled time

In 1911, Marie failed to be elected to the Academy of Sciences. Many people said that it was simply because she was a woman, since her scientific work was of the highest quality. Her personal life was followed by the newspapers, and there was great interest in her friendship with physicist colleague Paul Langevin, who had left his wife. Extremely upset by this public attention, Marie fell ill. After treatment, she stayed with her friend Hertha Ayrton in England.

When she returned to work in Paris in 1912, she was offered a special laboratory by the Pasteur Institute. Half of the building was for radiation research and the other half for the medical applications of radioactivity. Radium clinics were opening in many areas. Some made wild claims about what the magical radium could treat and cure. Radium institutes were also being founded for research into the medical and other uses of the precious radioactive metal.

By 1914, the Radium Institute at the University of Paris was finished. The same year, World War I began.

Chapter Six

The War and After

Marie Curie threw herself into the war effort. She obtained funds and arranged for X-ray equipment for hospitals, to help them locate bullets and shrapnel in the wounds of injured soldiers. She studied anatomy in her spare time and taught her daughter Irène to help. She set up a course to train people to use the radiography (X-ray) units.

At the end of the war, in 1918, Marie became Director of the Paris Radium Institute. Irène worked with her, studying the alpha particles given off by polonium. The Institute became a world center for radiation physics and chemistry. Under Marie's guidance, the researchers studied the chemistry of radioactive substances and their medical uses.

The vans in the picture, called "Little Curies," were World War I vehicles fitted with X-ray equipment. They were used to check injured soldiers near the battlefront for broken bones and embedded bullets. Marie and her helpers obtained and fitted 200 of these mobile X-ray units.

Marie and her daughter Irène, ready to help the injured of World War I. They asked the rich people of Paris to give funds for the war effort.

Marie takes the arm of U.S.
President Harding on her tour in
1921. On the far left is Marie
Meloney, Marie's journalist friend,
who organized and publicized this
tour (and many others). However,
Marie Curie often became tired
and ill, and she had to cut her
travels short. In the photograph
below, she is returning to Europe.

Tours and fund-raising

In 1920, at the age of 52, Marie Curie became friends with another Marie—Marie Meloney, an American journalist. Marie the journalist helped to improve the public image of Marie the scientist and planned to raise money for the Radium Institute by having Marie give a lecture tour in the U.S.

Although Marie Curie's hearing and sight were failing, she carried out part of the tour before illness forced her to return to France. American people and industries gave her money, samples of radioactive substances, and equipment. Many universities awarded her special degrees, and The Women of America gave her one gram of radium, worth one hundred thousand dollars, in recognition of her work and achievements as a woman scientist. The radium was presented by the American President Warren G. Harding.

In 1922, she was at last elected to the French Academy of Sciences.

The invisible danger

During the 1920s, the damaging effects of radioactivity on the human body—and on all living things—were becoming more obvious. Many "miracle" preparations containing radium, such as face creams and tonics, did more harm than good. The scientists who had worked with the Curies in the early years were ill and dying. Gradually the hazards of radioactivity—burns, ulcers, cancers, and many other illnesses—were recognized and guarded against.

The later years

Marie continued to oversee the work in her own laboratories in Paris. She also traveled to raise funds for research by younger scientists. She went to Belgium, Brazil, Spain, and Czechoslovakia. On a return visit to the U.S. in 1928, she was given a car by auto manufacturer Henry Ford, and she met President Herbert Hoover at the White House. She sent some of her money to the new Radium Institute in her hometown of Warsaw.

Marie had an operation for cataracts, a condition in which the lenses of the eyes become clouded. She was cared for by her daughter Ève, but after further illness, she died on July 4, 1934, in Sancellemoz, Switzerland. A pioneer of radioactivity research, and the first famous woman scientist, she had suffered from radiation sickness for more than half her life.

The case of the dial painters

During 1927–28, there was a famous court case in the United States. Five women whose jobs were to put the radium-based luminous paint onto clock dials were dying. They believed their illnesses were caused by exposure to the radioactive paint. They went to court against their employer, the U.S. Radium Corporation, and asked for money to pay for their medical treatment. The case made newspaper headlines worldwide. Marie Curie herself wrote to suggest that they eat raw calf's liver. The U.S. Radium Corporation said the paint was not the cause of the illnesses, but it gave money and pensions to the women.

The Curies are often depicted on postage stamps celebrating their discoveries and lives. The star-like picture on the far right is a diagram of an atom.

Chapter Seven
Marie Curie in Perspective

Marie's discovery, radium, is rarely used today, even in scientific research. However, her work on its purification, and on the nature of its emissions, helped enormously toward an understanding of radioactivity in general and the nature of the atom.

Atomic bombs

The work of Marie Curie, Ernest Rutherford, Albert Einstein, Otto Hahn, and many other scientists led to the understanding of the nature of atoms and how they can be split or joined to release energy. In nuclear fission, the nuclei of atoms are forced apart. In nuclear fusion, the nuclei fuse or join together. Under the right conditions, incredible amounts of heat, light, and other forms of energy are released.

Near the end of World War II, two atomic bombs of devastating power were dropped on Japan. The bombs worked by nuclear fission. Today, many countries have enough of the even more powerful hydrogen bombs, based on nuclear fusion, to destroy the world many times over.

A terrifying result of scientific research: The second atomic bomb explodes over the Japanese city of Nagasaki in 1945. Radioactivity was spread over a huge area. World War II ended a few days later.

The work of Irène and Frédéric

The Curie family carried on the research. In 1925, Marie's daughter Irène earned her doctor of science degree for research into the alpha rays emitted by polonium. Marie did not attend the ceremony so that Irène could receive all the attention. A year later, Irène married French physicist Frédéric Joliot, Marie's laboratory assistant. Their work at the Radium Institute in Paris led to the discovery of artificial radioactivity in 1934. (This phenomenon is caused when a nonradioactive substance is bombarded with emissions and itself becomes radioactive.) They bombarded aluminum with alpha rays from plutonium, creating a form of phosphorous. In 1935, Frédéric and Irène Joliot-Curie received the Nobel Prize for Chemistry.

The Joliot-Curies' work also contributed to the discovery of atomic particles called neutrons by English physicist James Chadwick, in 1932.

Marie's daughter Irène and her physicist husband Frédéric Joliot. They got to know one another when Frédéric was employed as Marie's laboratory assistant.

Nuclear power

In 1942, building on the work of the Curies and many other scientists, the physicist Enrico Fermi operated the first experimental nuclear reactor at the University of Chicago. The atomic or nuclear power station followed. Uranium is used as fuel to produce enormous quantities of heat, which is turned into electricity. As a uranium nucleus splits and gives off energy, its parts go on to split other uranium nuclei, in an ever-increasing chain reaction. A piece of uranium releases more than two million times as much heat as a piece of burning coal of the same size.

The process must be carefully controlled in a power station, to release energy at a steady rate. This is difficult to do, and it also produces various kinds of radioactive wastes. The radioactivity will last for thousands of years, and no one really knows what to do with the wastes or how to make them safe.

The terrible explosion at the Chernobyl power station in the Soviet Union in 1986 showed that radioactivity is still one of the world's greatest threats. We are still learning to control atomic processes and the dangers that go with them.

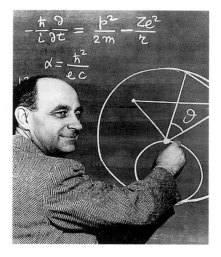

Enrico Fermi received the Nobel Prize for Physics in 1938, for his work on how substances change when they are bombarded by atomic particles.

Albert Einstein, one of the most famous scientists of all time. He worked mainly on theories, using mathematics and writing scientific articles, rather than doing experiments in the laboratory like the Curies. All these scientists, theorists, and experimenters helped greatly toward our modern understanding of atoms, radiation, and the forces of nature.

The World in Marie Curie's Time

	1850-1875	1876-1900
Science	**1859** Pierre Curie is born **1867** Marie Curie is born as Maria Sklodowska **1874** George Stoney introduces the term "electron" for an as yet unknown particle that he suspects exists	**1886** Chemist Alfred Nobel invents dynamite **1893** William Ramsay discovers a new chemical element, the rare gas argon **1893** Otto Lilienthal completes successful test flights in his new glider
Western Expansion and Exploration	**1869** The Suez Canal opens, connecting the Mediterranean Sea with the Red Sea and Indian Ocean	**1890** Cleopatra's tomb is discovered in Egypt **1893** Fridtjof Nansen sets sail from Norway for the North Pole
Politics	**1853** Crimean War begins in the Black Sea region **1861** American Civil War begins **1867** Karl Marx publishes *Das Kapital*	**1878** The Treaty of Berlin gives independence to Romania, Serbia, and Montenegro **1894** War breaks out between Japan and China **1900** Boxer Rebellion in China
Arts	**1862** Victor Hugo writes *Les Misérables* **1863** Edouard Manet paints *Luncheon on the Grass* **1865** Lewis Carroll publishes *Alice in Wonderland*	**1891** Sir Arthur Conan Doyle publishes *The Adventures of Sherlock Holmes* **1892** Henri Toulouse-Lautrec paints *At the Moulin Rouge* **1893** Antonín Dvořák completes his Symphony in E Minor, *From the New World*

1901-1925	1926-1950
1902 Rutherford and Soddy publish *The Cause and Nature of Radioactivity*	**1930** Karl Landsteiner wins a Nobel Prize for his discovery of human blood groups
1906 Pierre Curie dies	**1934** Marie Curie dies
1921 Frederick Banting and Charles Best work on a treatment for diabetes using insulin	**1935** A scale for measuring earthquakes is devised by Charles Richter
1906 Annie Smith Peck is the first person to reach the top of Huascarán, the highest peak in Peru	**1926** Richard Byrd is first to fly over the North Pole in an airplane
1915 The Panama Canal is opened in a great ceremony (though ships have been using it for a year)	**1933** The White Sea Canal, 140 mi. (225 km.) long, links the White and Baltic Seas
1911–12 Revolution in China; new republic forms	**1933** Hitler comes to power in Germany
1914–18 World War I	**1936** Spanish Civil War begins
1917 Bolshevik Revolution: Marxists overthrow Russian government	**1939** World War II begins
1922 Benito Mussolini takes power in Italy	**1945** Two atomic bombs dropped on Japan end World War II
1902 The great Italian singer Enrico Caruso makes his first gramophone recording	**1928** Walt Disney makes his first Mickey Mouse cartoon
1910 Black dance bands in Memphis, Tennessee, begin to bring their music to wider audiences	**1935** George Gershwin completes his opera *Porgy and Bess*
1913 Cecil B. De Mille makes one of his first films, *The Squaw Man*	**1937** Pablo Picasso paints *Guernica*

Glossary

alloy: a substance made by mixing two or more pure metals. Brass is an alloy of copper and zinc.

atoms: the smallest parts of a substance, far too tiny to see under the most powerful microscope. Atoms can be split into smaller particles, such as electrons and neutrons, but these no longer have the physical and chemical features and properties of the original substance. (See also *element*.)

chalcolite: a mineral that contains the metal copper and gives off radioactivity.

Davy Medal: a medal awarded for achievements in chemistry and science, named in honor of the English chemist Humphry Davy (1778–1829).

distill: to purify by heating a liquid to turn it into a gas or vapor, then cooling it so that it changes back to a liquid. The heating and cooling temperatures are chosen so that impurities are left behind.

electrically charged: when the atoms in an object have an uneven balance of protons and electrons and therefore have a negative or positive, instead of neutral, charge. A positively charged object loses electrons; a negatively charged object gains electrons.

electrolyze: to break down a liquid into its elements by passing electricity through it. This process is one way to purify substances.

electromagnetic: relating to magnetism developed by a current of electricity.

electromagnetic radiation: a series of electromagnetic waves, such as radio waves, light waves, X rays, and gamma rays.

electrometer: a scientific device for measuring how much electricity can pass through air or similar substances.

electron: a negatively charged particle that circles around the nucleus of an atom.

element: a single, pure substance, such as iron or carbon. All the atoms of an element are the same as each other, and different from the atoms of other elements.

emission: something given off by a substance or process. The sun emits heat and light. Radioactive substances emit radiation as invisible particles and waves.

equation: a mathematical or chemical sum containing an equals sign (=), in which the two sides balance or are equal.

evolution: the cumulative changes in animals and plants over a very long time.

governess: a woman who looks after and teaches children in their home.

laboratory: a place where people carry out scientific research and experiments.

mineral: a natural nonliving substance, such as stone, coal, salt, or sulphur, that comes from the earth.

mineralogy: the study of minerals.

neutron: a particle in the nucleus of an atom that has no electric charge.

Nobel Prizes: a group of prizes awarded each year for great achievements in physics, chemistry, physiology or medicine, economics, literature, and peace. They are named after Alfred Nobel (1833–1896), the Swedish chemist and manufacturer. The fortune made from his invention, dynamite, provides money for the prizes.

nuclear: to do with the nucleus, which is the central part of an atom.

ore: a natural, unpurified mixture of rocks and other substances as mined from the earth.

penetrate: to go into or even all the way through a substance. Light can penetrate water and glass, but not wood; X rays penetrate the flesh of the body, but they cannot penetrate bones.

positivists: people who view science and scientific facts as the most important source of our knowledge. Religions, traditions, legends, and myths are much less important to them.

property: in chemistry and physics, a trait of a substance, such as its color, shininess, hardness, and the temperature at which it melts or turns into a gas.

proton: a positively charged particle in the nucleus of an atom.

radioactivity: a property of some elements, such as uranium, of spontaneously emitting particles or rays. It is caused by the disintegration of the nuclei of atoms.

shrapnel: pieces of metal and other materials produced by an explosion, which fly off and cause damage.

suffragettes: the name given to women who campaigned for voting rights for women, in the times when their countries allowed only men to vote.

tuberculosis: a serious disease that affects the lungs and other body parts, causing severe coughing, fever, sweating, general ill health, and sometimes death.

uranium: a heavy, silvery-white metal that gives off radioactivity. It is an example of an element.

Index